Little One

Robert D. Malanga

Illustrated by Erin Schuetz

Text copyright © 2021 by Nina Malanga Robinett
Ilustrations copyright © 2021 by Erin Schuetz
Printed in USA

All rights reserved. No part of this book may be reproduced, transmitted, or stored in an information retrieval system in any form or by any means, graphic, electronic, or mechanical, including photocopying, taping, and recording, without prior written consent from publishers.

First Edition 2021

Issued in print format.
ISBN 978-0-578-92962-0

The illustrations in this book were done in watercolor
with digital painting and editing.
www.erinschuetz.com

For all the Little Ones.

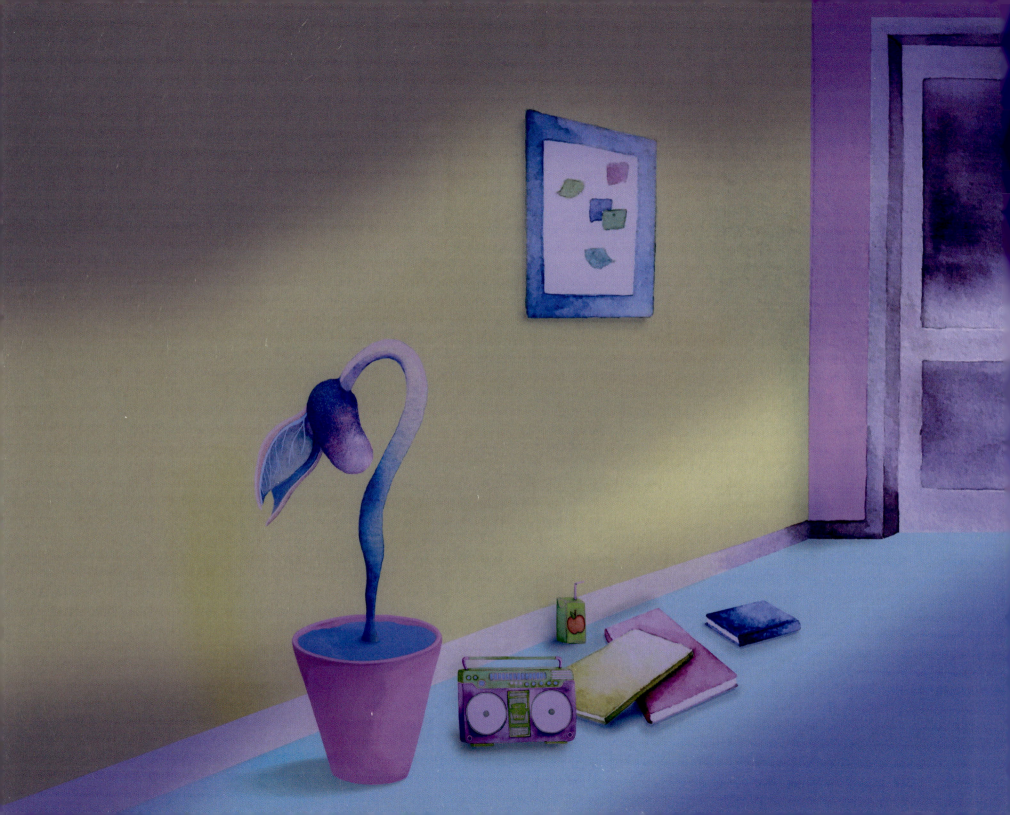

Bring with you
my Little One, a late night

happy thought

where you go.

And bring with you my Little One

For there, inside your mind, so far away

a world awaits

for you to come

and play.

And all the things that make you feel the best,

For **dreams** are **light** and nothing meant to fear, where you are safe and **love** is always near.

So bring with you my Little One,

And leave the cares you carried through the day

For twinkling starlit

dreams

that come your way.

And bring with you, my Little One

About the Author

Robert D. Malanga

Robert was born in Belleville, New Jersey in 1953. Although he was born with Cystic Fibrosis, he was determined to have fun, laugh often and live life to the fullest. He was a loving husband and father who cherished family above all else. He spent his life writing poetry, creating art, and in his later years was a full-time cartoonist for nationally published newspapers and magazines. In his free time, he enjoyed watching the NY Giants, snacking on Twinkies and taking trips down the shore. He is remembered for his infectious smile, witty sense of humor, and courage.

Robert passed away from CF in 2002, but his memory lives on through this poem, Little One, and in our hearts.

About the Illustrator

Erin Schuetz

Erin is an artist and teacher most recently living in NYC. Her creative work celebrates the many dimensions of the human experience. Through ideation she works to bring up the truth within us all. With keen intuitive and visual perception, the goal is activation and inspiration for the viewer. She is currently traveling and spending her days painting, reading, analyzing astrological transits and researching ancient cultures. She embraces the urban matrix as well as the healing vibrancy of the natural world.

After teaching visual arts for 13 years, Erin has embarked on a new path. She is now soul coaching through 'Aether Learning Laboratory.'

Thank you to all of our Kickstarter backers.
Your support brought Little One to life.